sisters

Sandra Deeble

with photography by Dan Duchars

sisters

RYLAND
PETERS
& SMALL
LONDON NEW YORK

For Laura Gibbons and Diana Marsh

Designer Catherine Griffin
Editor Miriam Hyslop
Location Research Claire Hector
Picture Research Emily Westlake
Production Deborah Wehner
Art Director Gabriella Le Grazie
Publishing Director Alison Starling

First published in the
United States in 2003
by Ryland Peters & Small
519 Broadway
5th Floor
New York NY 10012
www.rylandpeters.com

10 9 8 7 6 5 4 3 2

ISBN 1 84172 390 8

Printed and bound in China.

contents

*a friend
for life*

Your sister will always be your sister

Friends may come and go—however much they feel like permanent fixtures at the time—but sisters are there for the duration. Growing up with a sister is like having a ready-made friend, particularly if she's close to you in age. You're in an enviable position: you can afford to be lazy when it comes to making friends outside your own family. Early on, if friends let you down and can't come to play, you can always fall back on your sister. Knowing that she's there all the time when you're young can set a precedent for the rest of your life. Your sister is less likely to disown you, after all! So, while we're aware that friends demand a certain amount of maintenance, it's tempting to take a sister for granted. You can get away with not calling, with being thoughtless,

*We tell each other everything. With her,
it's no holds barred. She's my soulmate.
I'd be absolutely lost without her.*

Charlotte Pike

selfish, or downright nasty, because you know that she will forgive you. And however frank you might think you're being with friends, honesty reaches a different level between sisters. You can let it all out, and tell her things you'd probably be too ashamed to admit to your friends. She knows you so well that she's more likely to understand what you're talking about, without judging you. Not everyone's so lucky. If you wish that you were closer to your sister, it's probably because you have witnessed the most natural friendships that exist between

*For there is no friend
like a sister.*

Christina Rossetti

other sisters. Yet whatever relationship you have with your own sister you know that, when the chips are down, you can count on her. There is something compelling about sisters. If you're at a party with a close friend and a complete stranger asks you both: "Are you sisters?," you might feel flattered. The two of you are obviously emitting an aura of closeness: your relationship appears to be something out of the ordinary, something as special as sisterhood.

birth order

The middle one. The clever one.

It's not just an age thing. You were probably lucky or unlucky enough to earn your label early. You can try to fight it, but your place and your function in the family—be it based on when you arrived or certain attributes you displayed from birth—is something that you learn to live with.

Once you leave home and are a proper grownup, it becomes easier to be your own person. You'll feel less like the big or the little sister. Depending on what you're up to; you might find yourself looking up to your younger sister, just because she seems to have her life sorted out at a point when you might be floundering. Or maybe you both have children around the same time, and all of a sudden your defined role in the family becomes irrelevant. Just remember not to pigeonhole your own children! They won't thank you for it. With siblings, when it comes to who does what first, there are certain expectations. Whether it's passing your driving test, having your first sexual experience, or announcing that you're pregnant, it might seem old-fashioned, but it helps if the eldest paves the way. As one woman says candidly: "I think my sister would be quite upset if I had children before her." If you've always dreamed of having a sister after a lifetime of making do with only a brother, you might get very excited when he announces that he's getting married. At last! You're about to acquire a sister-in-law! Could she become like a real sister to you? This can work brilliantly, but there can be many disappointments. Similarly, a close friend might try to fix

Even now that we're grown up, I still feel incredibly protective of my little sister.

Diana Marsh

you up with her brother, saying hopefully: "And, if it all works out, we'll be sisters-in-law!" Sadly, this is often doomed to failure. Sometimes a half-sister or a stepsister can be seen

as a gift for an only child, or for a little girl who already has a brother. One woman remembers: "My mother brought home my new baby half-sister from the hospital, all wrapped up in a tight little bundle. I was absolutely thrilled." And another woman says: "I've got one sister and two

stepsisters, but if anyone asks about my family, I always say that I've got three sisters. I don't like the word 'step.' It makes me think of fairy tales like Cinderella and Snow White!"

*reliving
childhood*

The way we are brought up leaves an indelible mark on us

Values, the way we approach life, how we feel about things, can all be traced back to our upbringing. Rather than spending a fortune on therapy, a cheaper alternative might be talking to your sister. You can cut corners when you explain

things to her: you don't need to fill her in on your background!` And she might offer some interesting insights and even remember things that you had forgotten. Your sister is your childhood when it comes to play. Make-believe games, setting up stores, directing films. With a hairbrush for a microphone, it's relatively easy to form

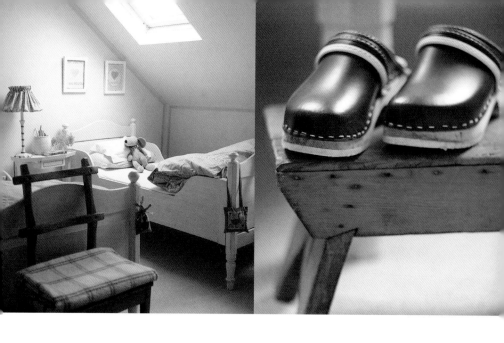

an all-girl singing group. Whether your role models are the Supremes or Destiny's Child, you can have fun without even leaving home. And you'll always be able to tap into that sense of joy. Shared bedrooms, often a source of discontent, are never forgotten. One sister remembers that, even after they'd

all graduated to separate rooms, they would still want to sleep over together, sometimes putting a mattress on the floor of each other's rooms, just to recreate some of that lights-out closeness of their early childhood. Years later, when you're grown up and you've both got children of your own, you can

I don't laugh with anybody else the way I do with my sister. We laugh at the most ridiculous things. I can't explain that.

Hazel Beynon

look back at some of the things you used to do together. Perhaps your own children will love spending the night with their cousins, reminding you of the fun you and your sister used to have when it should have been bedtime! Or at family get-togethers, Thanksgiving and birthdays, you will be comfortable to fall back into how you used to act with your sister when you were little.

chalk and cheese

You're just like your sister!

"You're nothing like your sister!" Whatever anyone says, as far as you're concerned, it probably falls short of the mark. Yet like it or not, there will be certain similarities. Your voice. A smile. A gesture. A reaction to a situation. Have you ever done something and found yourself thinking: "My sister does that"? Whether it's how you look or what you do, you're always going to be compared—or you will compare yourself—to her. You just can't get away from it. Your parents shouldn't set you up against each other, but as we all know, they're not perfect, so it happens.

I don't try to compete anymore. When we go out, the attention is always on my middle sister because she's so beautiful. But I've got other things that she hasn't got.

Beth Stimpson

And if you were at the same school, you'll know how infuriating it is to be told: "Oh, I see it runs in the family." You might sound the same on the telephone, a fact that makes

My older sisters used to tell me that I was really a movie star's daughter but that she had given me away because I was so ugly and mom had taken me in because she felt sorry for me.

Beth Stimpson

one sister say: "It's really spooky when I hear her voice on the answering machine: it's like listening to myself." As for identical twin sisters, the temptation to confuse boyfriends is hard to resist. When it comes to making decisions in life, you

We're from the same parents but all so different.

Valerie Eldred

might sometimes wonder what your sister would do, before calling her to ask for advice. Your sister can act as a barometer for your reactions. Knowing that there is someone else in the world so similar to you in many ways, a person you know inside out, can give you a feeling of empowerment. Together, you have something unique, which other people might envy.

chalk and cheese 39

is that my shirt you're wearing?

Having a sister offers immediate access to an extended wardrobe

Unauthorised borrowing is inadvisable, but it goes with the territory. You can probably remember an occasion—or several—when you ran out of the house quickly, hoping against hope that the illicitly worn favorite black top wouldn't get spotted. While you're out, feeling pretty damn confident, the compliment "I like your top" might cause a twinge of guilt, but hey! it's worth it. And that's before you've addressed the challenge of how to get the item back into the closet before it's missed. If you're planning to put in a request for something, you might have to build up to it over a few days

We occasionally try to sneak things away without asking, but then you get a phone call saying: "Where's my top?"

Charlotte Pike

by being extra nice, yet without arousing suspicion. Ask any sister, and she'll swear blind that she wasn't the worst offender: it was always her sister who did the most borrowing. And most of the time without asking first. Years later, when you're wearing your boyfriend's sweater, you're reminded of the intimacy of sharing and wearing your sister's clothes. You may even miss those days. Oh, come on, get real, it annoyed the hell out of you at the time! And when it comes to looking through old family photos, there's nothing worse than seeing you and your sister in matching outfits. Identical

twins are likely to suffer this more than most! Yet while some sisters go through phases of not wanting anyone to know that they come from the same family, there are times when putting on a sister act can be fun. One woman remembers going to visit her younger sister at college: she would wear her sister's fashionable ra-ra skirts over black leggings when they went out. And whenever her sister came to the city to visit, she would take on the mantle of her older sister:

wellworn suede jackets and ripped jeans. More poignantly, the youngest of three recalls the day when she asked her mother: "Is this dress really for me? But it can't be: it's brand new!" after a lifetime of wearing hand-me-downs.

sparks fly

Does your sister drive you nuts?

Does she know how to wind you up like nobody else? Can she irritate you beyond words? The closer you are to your sister, the easier it is to upset her. While the love you feel for your sister might be overwhelming at times, there is always a flip side. One minute you might want to kill her. Yet the minute someone wrongs her, you'd kill for her. When you do have an argument, or even when you feel one brewing, there is all that old, old stuff that comes back to haunt you. Remember the time when she threw your dolls out of the window? Or the day when she scribbled all over one of your favorite books? While it might seem ridiculous to dredge up these memories, like it or not, they'll pop up when you least expect them. But you're adults now! You should be able to be more rational,

There was some real Joan Collins
Dynasty stuff: fighting, pulling hair . . .

Beth Stimpson

> *Never praise a sister to a sister, in the hope of your compliments reaching the proper ears.*

Rudyard Kipling

more mature! Nevertheless, having a barney with your sister can cause the deepest of rifts. Some sisters fall out famously: Hilary and Jacqueline du Pré; Joan Fontaine and Olivia de Havilland; Margaret Drabble and A. S. Byatt. Fortunately sisters usually find it within themselves to forgive each other. Don't feel bad about quarreling with your sister: even Laura and Mary Ingalls fell out at times.

an

unbreakable

bond

When push comes to shove, sisters will always stick together.

"We are family," sang Sister Sledge, in a "don't-mess-with-us" kind of a way. At times, the exclusive union between sisters has a power that goes way beyond the old "blood is thicker than water" adage. Brothers who have two sisters often say that they feel left out. They're not privy to the emotional shorthand shared by their female siblings. Adult sisters can often find it easier to keep in more regular contact with each other than with their brother, which is why he might

complain of being the last one to hear family news. And even parents can sometimes feel on the periphery. Two daughters seem well placed to become the most natural allies within a family. Your sister probably knows more about you than anyone else in the world as it is. When you want to vent your

A close sister is like having the best kind of mate on tap.

Laura Gibbons

spleen about your parents, who do you pick up the phone to? You can say the vilest things, safe in the knowledge that they'll be taken in context. Inevitably, we all end up being parents to our own parents. Just as they spent years ferrying us around, and worrying about us, one day the roles are reversed. You'll find yourself taking your parents to the airport and

meeting them after their holiday. Perhaps your mom will want you to help her choose a dress for a special occasion, or even act as her "partner" at an event. Being able to share this responsibility with your sister is heaven-sent. However much you might try to be the perfect daughter, there are times when your parents will drive you mad, partly because you're in denial: you don't want to admit to yourself that they're getting older. If you're lucky, you and your sister can work as a team, dividing up parental duties and also making good use of each other when you want to have a moan, then later, as usually happens, to offload guilt! A word of warning: if your close friend has a sister, think very carefully before joining in when she has a whinge about her sibling. You'll soon be put in your place. You're only a friend, after all. And "she's my sister" will always resonate far more than "she's my friend."

The best thing about having a sister is being able to share the big, life-changing, gut-wrenching things: first seriously broken heart, marriage, the birth of a first child. Feeling jealous is par for the course: where are you in all of this? You're suddenly demoted to second place. But you'll find it in yourself to put your own doubts and insecurities to one side. The thing is, you're hell-bent on making sure that your sister is doing OK.

Beth is my conscience, and I can't give her up. I can't! I can't!

Louisa M. Alcott
Spoken by Jo March in *Little Women*

picture credits & acknowledgments

Key: **a**=above, **b**=below, **r**=right, **l**=left, **c**=center, **ph**= photographer
All photography by **Dan Duchars** taken at Janie Jackson's house in London
(unless stated otherwise)
For specific products contact:
Janie Jackson, Parma Lilac t. +44 (0)20 8960 9239, f. +44 (0)20 7912 0993
info@parmalilac.co.uk www.parmalilac.co.uk

3 ph Polly Wreford; **4 ph** Sandra Lane; **5 ph** Tom Leighton;
8–9 ph Debi Treloar; **11 ph** Caroline Arber; **12–13 ph** Jan Baldwin;
13 ph Jan Baldwin; **16–17 ph** Debi Treloar/Ben Johns & Deb Waterman Johns'
house in Georgetown; **20 ph** Christopher Drake; **21 ph** Craig Fordham;
24–25 ph Debi Treloar; **26 ph** Debi Treloar/Sue & Lars-Christian Brask's house in
London designed by Susie Atkinson Design, tel. 0468 814134;
27 ph Christopher Drake/Designer Barbara Davis' own house in upstate
New York; **30 ph** Polly Wreford; **32 a** Debi Treloar; **32 b ph** Polly Wreford;
34–35 ph Debi Treloar; **38–40 ph** Polly Wreford; **42 ph** Tom Leighton;
44 ph Polly Wreford/Paper flower by Libby Lister, tel. 01460 64605;
45 ph Polly Wreford/Ros Fairman's house in London; **46 ph** Christopher Drake;
47 ph Polly Wreford; **56–57 ar ph** Polly Wreford; **57 br ph** Caroline Arber;
60 ph Debi Treloar; **61 ph** Peter Cassidy; **62 ph** James Merrell

In addition to those mentioned above, we would like to thank our models Chloe,
Laura, Georgina, and Lucy.
The author would like to thank all the sisters who helped with this book.